# The GOALIE'S SECRET

## PAUL SHIPTON

### Illustrated by John Bendall-Brunello

Oxford University Press

## OXFORD
UNIVERSITY PRESS

Great Clarendon Street, Oxford OX2 6DP

Oxford University Press is a department of the University of Oxford.
It furthers the University's objective of excellence in research, scholarship,
and education by publishing worldwide in

Oxford New York

Auckland Bangkok Buenos Aires Cape Town Chennai
Dar es Salaam Delhi Hong Kong Istanbul Karachi Kolkata
Kuala Lumpur Madrid Melbourne Mexico City Mumbai Nairobi
São Paulo Shanghai Taipei Tokyo Toronto

Oxford is a registered trade mark of Oxford University Press
in the UK and in certain other countries

First published 1996
20 19 18 17 16 15 14 13 12 11

ISBN 0 19 916914 4  School edition

Printed in the UK by Goodmanbaylis
Illustrations by John Bendall-Brunello

# 1

# Things look bad

The ref blew hard on his whistle.
PEEP!

That *peep* meant bad news for Phil
'Sneezy' Naylor. It was a penalty for
the other side.

Phil stood alone on the goal-line.
The rest of the Milton Road Juniors 11
watched grimly. Phil had already let
four goals in.

They called him 'Sneezy' because, after one terrible game, someone had joked 'the only thing he could catch was a cold'. It was true – Phil wasn't very good.

The striker ran up and kicked the ball. Phil started to go one way,

... then changed his mind and went the other.

He fell over just as the ball shot into the back of the net. Goal!

Phil's team-mates all let out a sigh, as if to say: 'Sneezy's let us down again.' Kevin, the captain, shook his head.

Jimmy Seaton, who was Phil's only friend on the team, tried to cheer him up.

Never mind – I bet that ball was doing about fifty miles an hour.

Jimmy had an annoying habit of guessing the speed of every shot.

I mean, no one would have made that save.

Phil nodded – that was just what he felt like: no one.

# 2

# Disaster!

Phil was in a terrible mood as he
walked home through the park. The
rest of the team had gone round to
Kevin's house after the game. But Kev
had not asked Phil to go.

And Phil knew why... he had let the
team down again. He was just no
good! He felt like kicking himself, but
instead he booted the ball. All of his
anger went into it, and it was a good,
hard kick.

The ball went high and zoomed out over the park railings, across the street and straight into the garden of the house opposite.

It could have bounced against the wall and rolled safely down the drive. It didn't.

It could have landed on the lawn. It didn't. The ball crashed straight through a greenhouse in front of the house.

A dog began howling from inside the house. Then the front door opened and an old lady in pink slippers darted out. A small dog followed at her heels.

Her eyes moved from the broken glass to the football, and then over to Phil. He wished that life was like a video and he could rewind the last couple of minutes.

The old woman pointed one finger at him.

# 3

## Mary Frost

The woman gave him a stern look as she scooped the ball up.

Phil hung his head. Mum and Dad would be mad when they found out about this. They'd make him pay for it out of his own money.

I'm really sorry. Will it cost a lot to fix it?

When the woman told him, he hung his head even lower. Even counting all his savings and pocket money, he would have to get a paper round to pay for this.

The old woman was staring at him. She said sharply, 'Hold on, I know who you are. You play for that Milton Road team, don't you?'

Phil nodded glumly.

The woman cut him off. She said, 'I know what you are. I've watched you play, and I can only say one thing: what *is* the world coming to? Eh, Rex?'

Rex thought this over with a growl. Phil felt his face go red.

'I'll tell you,' said the woman. 'I can see you love football. But that's not enough – you've got to love being a *goalie*, which is a different thing altogether.'

Phil was beginning to feel angry. Wasn't it enough that his team thought he was useless?

Suddenly a big grin appeared on the old woman's face.

Still wearing her pink slippers and with the ball under her arm, she marched across the road. Like the dog Rex, Phil followed behind her.

Once they were in the park, she rolled the ball toward Phil.

Phil couldn't believe his ears. But he didn't want to argue with her. Not after the greenhouse. Feeling silly, he tapped the ball towards her.

The old lady kicked it straight back.

Phil felt a flare of anger. He took another shot, and this time it was a good one. It was a chip which he thought would sail over the old lady's head.

But the woman began to run backwards. She was fast for someone with such short legs. Her eyes never left the ball.

At exactly the right moment, she jumped into the air. She grabbed the football with one hand and pulled it down.

She had saved it!

Phil just stood there in shock. The old lady grinned at him, while Rex ran excited laps around her ankles.

'My name's Mary Frost,' she said, still grinning, 'and here's my idea. If you let me coach you for one week, I'll turn you into a good goalie. Or at least a halfway good goalie, eh, Rex?'

Phil didn't know what to say.

Suddenly she looked serious. 'But you have to agree to do everything I tell you,' she said. 'No moaning or silly questions.'

Phil's mind was racing. What would the rest of the team think if they saw him training with this odd old lady?

Before he could say anything, Mary
Frost spoke again.

Phil didn't know what to do. He
didn't want this woman coaching
him, even if she *had* just made a lucky
save. But then he thought of how
much the glass would cost. You didn't
have to be brilliant at maths to work
out it would take ages to pay off.

At last he nodded.

Mrs Frost beamed.

'Good!' she said. 'I'll expect you here in the park first thing in the morning. I'm going to make you a goalie!'

Phil gave a weak smile and wondered, *What have I got myself into?*

The old lady grinned as if she could read his mind.

# 4

# Things get worse

Part of Phil hoped that his mum would say he couldn't go, but she didn't. 'That's fine,' she said. 'I know Mrs Frost – I see her at the shop sometimes.' Then she'd winked. 'She's football crazy, just like you.' So that was that.

Training began early the next morning.

Phil was wearing a pair of welly boots two sizes too big, and boxing gloves.

Mrs Frost tut-tutted.

Now, now.
Remember the deal —
no questions.

Phil had remembered. That's why he
hadn't said anything when they had
come to the tennis courts. Or when
Mrs Frost told him to put the boots
and gloves on.

*Or* when she had pulled a tennis
racquet and tennis balls out of her bag.

'Okay,' said Mrs Frost. 'Stand over there. I want you to catch these tennis balls... (if you can, eh, Rex?)'

The dog said nothing.

Once Phil was far enough away, Mrs Frost hit a tennis ball at him. It bounced off his chest.

She hit another, which whizzed past him.

It went on for ages. It was impossible to catch the balls. He could hardly move in the over-sized wellies. And he could hardly catch anything in those boxing gloves. *And* Mrs Frost hit the ball a lot harder than he expected. Phil's arms and legs ached. And all the time he kept thinking: *I hope nobody sees me like this.*

Then something amazing happened.
Phil caught one.

But Mrs Frost was already packing
the racquet and balls back into her
bag.

'That's all for today,' she said. 'It's
nearly time for *East Street* on TV. That's
Rex's favourite programme, you know.
Can't stand it myself.'

Phil trailed behind as she marched
back to her house.

Before she went inside, she turned
to him.

Mrs Frost thought this over, then
said, 'Same time tomorrow. Come to
the house this time.'

# 5

# What is a goalie for?

rat-a-tat-tat

Mrs Frost was at the door almost
before Phil knocked.

This time she led him round to her
back garden. Phil was glad he didn't
have to wear wellies today. But then
he saw what was going to happen
instead.

Mrs Frost stood by a dustbin. But
there wasn't rubbish in it – there were
balloons.

*Lots* of balloons, all filled with water. Phil didn't like the look of this.

Mrs Frost said, 'All I want you to do is to catch these balloons. Simple, eh, Rex?'

She picked one up and lobbed it towards Phil. He jumped backwards. The balloon burst over his feet.

She tossed another one. Phil tried to catch it and it exploded against his chest, soaking him with water.

It was another fifteen balloons before Phil got the hang of it. He was drenched. The trick was to catch the balloon with arms stretched out, then pull it back to your chest.

After Phil had caught five in a row, a
tiny smile appeared on Mrs Frost's
face.

Ten minutes later Phil was in front
of the fire, sipping hot chocolate.
Mrs Frost sat opposite.

Phil blinked. Was this a trick question?

Erm ... to stop the ball going in the net?

Mrs Frost shook her head. She looked serious.

'No – not to stop the ball, to SAVE it,' she said. 'The goalie's job is saving things – saving the ball and saving the game. That's why a good goalie is a hero!'

*Great*, thought Phil – *but what have tennis balls and balloons got to do with it?* But, like Rex, he said nothing.

# 6

# Phil loses his temper

The next morning Phil found it hard
to get out of bed. What was the point
– to catch more tennis balls and
balloons?

But he knew he had to. Otherwise
he would have to find a lot of money.
He swung his legs out of bed.

When he arrived, Mrs Frost was at
the door as quickly as ever. She was
holding something in her hands.

It looked like an old mattress. In fact, it WAS an old mattress, but Mrs Frost had chopped and changed it to make a kind of suit. A great, big, padded suit.

'Come along now, chop, chop!' said Mrs Frost. 'We haven't got all day, have we, Rex?'

So that was how Phil found himself waddling into the back garden wearing a huge suit made out of a mattress.

Phil was puzzled.

Mrs Frost shook her head.

And so Phil spent the next two hours just leaping and diving onto the ground in his big, padded mattress suit. And all the time, he kept thinking, *I feel stupid!*

Another hour? That was it – Phil had had enough. He got up slowly. He would have jumped up, only he couldn't. He began yanking the mattress off.

Mrs Frost and Rex watched him pull off the last bit of the home-made suit.

'I mean, I haven't even caught a football since we started!' said Phil angrily. 'I think I'd rather pay for that window.'

Mrs Frost let out a long sigh. So did Rex. At last she spoke.

She ran into the house. She came back with two footballs, which she placed on the grass.

It was a good shot, especially as she still had her slippers on. But Phil hopped to the side, put himself behind the ball and hugged it tight to his chest. A save!

This was an even better shot, but Phil dived left and stopped it.

As he lay on the ground, still gripping the ball, he saw Mrs Frost grinning down at him.

And that's when he understood. All the exercises he thought were so daft... His reactions were much better and he had learned how to hold on to the ball. *And* he had learned how to dive without being afraid.

He rolled the ball back with a smile.

Mrs Frost did a little hop of
excitement.

# 7

# The most important lesson

Over the next few days, Phil worked hard, and he listened carefully. He no longer questioned anything. He practised jumping for high balls, and cutting down angles and punching the ball out with both fists.

Once, during a break, he asked Mrs Frost, 'How come you know so much about being a goalie?'

Mrs Frost smiled. 'I've ALWAYS loved football,' she said. 'When I was young, there weren't any women's teams, but I played during breaks at the factory. That's where I met Stanley.'

She dug around in her handbag and pulled out a black-and-white photo.

Then she winked at Phil and jumped up.

Mary Frost looked him right in the eyes, and her face was more serious than he had ever seen.

# 8

# What will everyone think?

Phil ran into Jimmy during break-time.

Jimmy looked puzzled. 'I thought I saw you the other day near the park,' he said. 'You were wearing some kind of weird suit and jumping all over the place.'

Phil just shook his head.

Wasn't me.

It LOOKED like you. There was an old lady too, wearing pink slippers. And a dog...

Phil glanced at his watch.

I've got to go. See you at the game tomorrow.

He ran off, but as he ran a horrible thought popped into his head: what would everyone think if Mrs Frost came to cheer him on? Mrs Frost with her pink slippers and her loud voice and her dog?

The thought stayed in his mind all day like an unwelcome guest. It was still there during his final practice session.

Mrs Frost thought it must be nerves before the game.

Not to worry, lad. What time's kick-off? Rex and I want a good spot.

Oh... I... er... It's an away match.

No problem. I can take the bus.

Phil felt his cheeks go red.

No ... It's a long way away. There isn't a bus.

Mrs Frost went quiet.
Then she gave a little smile.

Oh, well... Rex and I have got things to do anyway. Eh, Rex?

No!

# 9

# The match

Right before the match, one of the defenders said, 'Make an effort this time, Sneezy.'

Phil ignored him. The nerves in his stomach felt more like buffaloes than butterflies. The game began.

After ten minutes the other team
made a break. The forward dribbled
the ball past two defenders and shot at
goal. Phil hopped up and caught the
ball safely.

The rest of his team were stunned.
Sneezy Naylor had saved a goal!
Jimmy looked as amazed as the rest.

Phil just smiled to himself. But then he realized – there was just one thing missing. He wished Mrs Frost was here. Why had he been so daft? Who cared what everyone else thought? After all, Mrs Frost had made him into a goalkeeper. More than that, she was his friend.

What's more, he realized, she probably needed a friend herself. She had always been so quick to answer the door. Maybe she was lonely? Phil made a promise to himself that he would put things right. And then he forced himself to concentrate on the game again.

For the rest of the match Phil made
save after save. The other team were
better, but they didn't score because
Phil was always there. With a couple
of minutes to go, the score was nil-nil.

But then disaster… A player ran
forward with the ball. He was fast and
Jimmy panicked. He tried to tackle,
missed the ball and brought the striker
down.

FOUL!

The referee blew for a penalty.

The player taking the penalty was
well known for never missing. The
whole Milton Road team looked as if
the game was over. Only Phil stayed
calm.

He stood alone on the goal-line, but he no longer felt lonely. He felt like a hero – his team's last line of defence. Everything rested on him, and he knew it.

The whistle blew and the striker ran forward.

Phil emptied his mind. He didn't even think which way to jump, he just watched the striker's eyes, like Mrs Frost had told him.

Suddenly everything was a blur. The ball was zooming through the air and Phil was diving for it.

It was a perfect dive. He stretched out one arm. His fingertips touched the ball and flicked it upwards.

The ball hit the crossbar with a thud and then… went in.
It was a goal.

# 10

# 'The best goalie around'

Phil couldn't believe it. He had been so close. But 'close' didn't count – a goal was a goal. He had let his team down again.

The last few minutes were a blur to him. When the final whistle sounded, he hung his head.

But then something amazing happened. His team-mates ran up and began to slap him on the back.

You played brilliantly, Phil. Nearly saved that penalty even!

If it hadn't been for you we'd have lost six-nil.

Kev, the captain, ran up too.

Hey, Phil, great game! Do you want to come round to my house later?

Phil grinned.

Thanks, but not this time, I'm going to see a good friend of mine.

# About the author

When I was growing up in Manchester, I always wanted to be an astronaut, a footballer, or (if those didn't work out for any reason) perhaps a rock star. So it came as something of a shock when I became first a teacher and then an editor of educational books.

I have lived in Cambridge, Aylesbury, Oxford and Istanbul. I'm still on the run and now live in Chicago with my wife and family.

If there really is a secret to being a good goalie, you won't find it in this book. Just practise lots!

**Other Treetops books at this level include:**

*I Wish, I Wish* by Paul Shipton
*The Personality Potion* by Alan MacDonald
*The Ultimate Trainers* by Paul Shipton
*Waiting for Goldie* by Susan Gates
*The Case of the Smiling Shark* by Tessa Krailing

**Also available in packs**
*Stage 13 pack B*          0 19 916918 7
*Stage 13 class pack B*    0 19 916919 5